QUARTZ HILL 110 DATE		SEP 14 2001	

ELIZABETH BLACKWELL

ELIZABETH BLACKWELL

The First Woman Doctor

IRA PECK

A Gateway Biography
The Millbrook Press
Brookfield, Connecticut

Published by The Millbrook Press, Inc.
2 Old New Milford Road
Brookfield, Connecticut 06804
www.millbrookpress.com

Library of Congress Cataloging-in-Publication Data
Peck, Ira.
Elizabeth Blackwell : the first woman doctor / Ira Peck.
p. cm. – (A Gateway biography.)
Includes bibliographical references and index.
Summary: A biography of Elizabeth Blackwell, the first woman to attend medical
school and practice medicine in the United States, and also discussing her careers in
Paris and London, and the medical colleges she helped establish.
ISBN 0-7613-1854-2 (lib. bdg.: alk. paper)
1. Blackwell, Elizabeth, 1821-1910. 2. Women physicians–Biography. [1. Blackwell,
Elizabeth, 1821-1910. 2. Physicians. 3. Women–Biography.] I. Title. II. Series.
R154.B623 P43 2000
610'.92–dc21 [B] 99-059796

Cover photograph courtesy of The Granger Collection, New York
Photographs courtesy of © NYU Downtown Hospital: p. 8; The Schlesinger Library,
Radcliffe Institute: pp. 9, 37; Archive Photos: pp. 11, 29; © Bettmann/Corbis: pp. 14,
17; Archives & Special Collections on Women in Medicine, MCP Hahnemann
University: pp. 20, 31 (both), 39; Dora Weiner: p. 22; New York Public Library Picture
Collection: p. 24; © Hulton Getty/Liaison Agency: p. 25; © Corbis: p. 33;
National Library of Medicine: p. 35.

ELIZABETH BLACKWELL

January 23, 1849, was a day that would forever change the world of medicine. On that day, students at the Geneva College of Medicine in upstate New York would graduate. Each would receive a diploma and the title of "Doctor." Of these students, 129 were men. One was a woman. She was special. She was about to become the very first woman doctor of modern times!

After all the men received their diplomas, the president of the college called out her name—"Elizabeth Blackwell." Elizabeth rose to receive her diploma. The president told the audience that she had graduated first in her class. As he handed Elizabeth her diploma, the audience cheered. Elizabeth blushed a deep red. Then she said, "Sir, I thank you. . . . It shall be the effort of my life to shed honor on this diploma."

Not only was Elizabeth Blackwell the first woman to attend and graduate from medical school, she was first in her class.

Elizabeth had a lot to be thankful for. She had asked many medical schools to admit her as a student. But until Geneva accepted her, all of them had said "No." Why? At that time, women were looked on as "the weaker sex." Most people believed that a woman's place was in the home, raising children, cooking, and cleaning. Many women, however, felt they were treated as servants and resented it.

Medical schools turned women away for other reasons. In those days, for example, many people felt that it

Elizabeth Blackwell's diploma from Geneva College of Medicine.

was not proper for a woman to study the human body. It was even wrong for women to talk about the body and diseases. How, then, could women become doctors?

Despite these popular beliefs, Elizabeth Blackwell did "shed honor" on her diploma throughout her career. Her example made it possible for thousands of women to become doctors. It wasn't easy. She had to battle constantly against male doctors who wanted to keep women out of their profession. But the more they tried to stop Elizabeth, the harder she fought them. And in the end she won. All women doctors today can thank her for that.

Elizabeth Blackwell was born in Bristol, England, a busy seaport, on February 3, 1821. She was the third daughter in a family of nine children. Tiny at birth, she never grew taller than 5 feet, 1 inch (155 centimeters). At first her parents, Samuel and Hannah Blackwell, weren't sure she would survive. But Elizabeth hung on and grew into a healthy child.

Samuel and Hannah Blackwell were deeply religious people. They had met at Bristol's Methodist Church where they were both Sunday school teachers. They raised their children to have the same strong religious faith as they did. They read the Bible and prayed at home as well as at church. Elizabeth read about the lives of saints and tried to imitate them. The saints had endured many hardships. On winter nights Elizabeth would sometimes sleep on the cold floor of her room. At other times she would give up eating for days. These hardships, she hoped, would make her body and soul stronger.

Yet Elizabeth was a happy girl. Although Samuel, her father, was sternly religious, he was affectionate toward

*A view of Bristol, England, around the time
Elizabeth Blackwell was born.*

his children. He also had a good sense of humor and liked to write funny poems to amuse them. Hannah Blackwell was a gentle woman, who also taught her children the importance of faith. Samuel owned a prosperous sugar refinery and could well afford to support his large family. The Blackwells lived in a fine home with a garden and open fields nearby. They could also afford a number of servants to do housework.

This pleasant life came to an end in 1831. Hard times had come to England. Many workers lost their jobs. Soon angry mobs began to riot in Bristol. They set fire to buildings and fought soldiers sent to stop them. When the rioting ended, 12 people were dead and almost 100 injured. The Blackwell family was deeply upset by the violence. The sugar refinery was still standing, but Samuel saw little hope of saving his business. To do so, he would have to borrow money, and he hated to be in debt. The best thing to do, he said, was to make a fresh start in America. In the land of opportunity, he thought, all would be well.

In August 1832 the family set sail for New York aboard a small ship. It took almost two months to reach New York. Most of the passengers were seasick. Elizabeth was also at times, but she seemed to enjoy herself. Later she wrote that sailing was a "delightful experience to the younger travelers." The Blackwells settled into a small house in lower Manhattan. Soon after,

Hannah Blackwell gave birth to her last child, a boy. He was named George Washington Blackwell in honor of the father of their new country, but everyone called him "Washy" for short.

By now Samuel was ready to start operating a sugar refinery near the waterfront. There was only one problem: The family needed more space. Blackwell found a larger house in Jersey City, across the Hudson River from Manhattan. There Elizabeth enjoyed ice skating, sleigh riding, fishing, and horseback riding. She also practiced playing the piano. There were no schools yet in Jersey City, so Elizabeth rode a ferry to Manhattan to attend schools there.

Samuel Blackwell's sugar refinery in Manhattan did a good business, but in 1836 a fire destroyed it. Blackwell got no help from his insurance company because it had no money to give him. Now life at home became bleak. All the servants were let go. The Blackwell girls had to do most of the housework themselves. Elizabeth hated cooking, especially when there was so little food. Once she wrote in her diary: "We had no meat for dinner yesterday. Today we had a stew (made up) of potatoes and a few bones. . . ." At night there was no oil to light the lamps. Elizabeth had to give up her piano lessons, which had meant so much to her.

Samuel Blackwell became more and more gloomy. Then one day a cousin from Ohio came for a visit. He told Blackwell that Ohio had the perfect climate for growing sugar beets. The roots of these beets could be refined and used as a sweetener. The cousin urged Blackwell to move to Ohio and go into business there. Blackwell liked the idea at once. The cane sugar that he refined came from big plantations in the West Indies where all the hard work was done by slaves. The entire Blackwell family was against slavery. Growing sugar beets in Ohio meant that Samuel Blackwell would not have to depend on slaves.

In the spring of 1838 the Blackwells started out for Cincinnati, Ohio. The nine-day trip was made mainly by stagecoaches and riverboats. Elizabeth liked Cincinnati.

The Blackwell family hoped for better times in Cincinnati, Ohio. They may have seen this very street upon their arrival in 1838.

THE ABOLITIONISTS

Samuel's opposition to slavery led him to join the abolitionist movement, the aim of which was to free all slaves. He became a supporter of William Lloyd Garrison, who was the founder of the American Anti-Slavery Society. Garrison often visited the Blackwell home. The abolitionists were almost as unpopular in the North as they were in the South. Many Northerners thought the abolitionists were fanatics. Those opposed to abolitionism were afraid that freed slaves would take jobs away from white people. Angry white mobs sometimes attacked abolitionist speakers and newspaper offices.

Members of the Blackwell family were threatened by violence on more than one occasion. Once an abolitionist minister named Samuel Cox made a remark in a sermon that angered many white people. Soon a mob was marching on Cox's home, threatening to hang him.

Cox quickly put his family into a carriage and raced to the home of his friend, Samuel Blackwell, where they were welcomed warmly. Elizabeth and her sisters gave up their rooms to the minister's five children. The Blackwell girls moved into the attic, which was small and very hot. They slept on the floor, proud that they could help the abolitionist cause. They did this for two weeks until it was safe for the Cox family to return home.

It was a neat, busy town, and the people were friendly. Samuel Blackwell rented a large house and a mill to start a sugar refinery. Everything seemed to be going well. But that summer Samuel became sick with a high fever and died within days. Elizabeth had always been her father's favorite child, and she took his death hard. She wrote: "I felt as though all hope and joy were gone. I seemed alone in the world."

When Samuel Blackwell died, he had only $20. He owed much more money than that. How would his family live? Where would they get money for food and to pay bills? Elizabeth was only 17, but she showed the way. She began by giving piano lessons. Before long, she opened a boarding school at home with her two older sisters. It was called the Cincinnati English and French Academy for Young Ladies. The sisters worked long hours. They gave courses in reading, writing, drawing, arithmetic, grammar, history, composition, and French. All this cost only $50 a year. Piano, harp, and guitar lessons could be obtained for another $50. Room and board cost $200 a year. It was hard work for the three sisters, but Elizabeth wrote: "We managed to support the family and maintain a home."

Teaching was one of the few jobs open to women at that time, but Elizabeth disliked it and wished that she could give it up. She was only 17 when she began and was afraid of her pupils. "The elder girls," she wrote, "were very wild western young women, utterly unaccustomed to discipline. I only controlled them by a steady quietness . . . which they took for sternness, but which was really fear."

A sick friend, Mary Donaldson, made Elizabeth think about another career. Mary had always admired Elizabeth for being so bright. Now she asked her, "Why don't you study medicine?" Elizabeth was shocked. She told her friend that she hated everything connected with the body. She could not bear the sight of a medical book. (Most proper young women of her time felt the same way.) Then Mary told Elizabeth why it was so important to have female doctors:

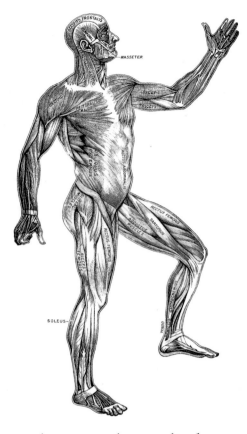

As they are today, medical books of the early nineteenth century were full of pictures of the human body and its systems. But in those days, it was unthinkable for a young woman to view pictures like this.

Many women were too shy to let male doctors examine them. Often they would wait to visit a doctor until it was too late. That was true of Mary Donaldson.

Elizabeth thought about her friend's idea for a long time. More and more it began to seem like the answer to her problems. Marriage did not appeal to her. She was very independent, and in those days a wife's first duty was to serve and obey her husband. She was determined, she wrote, "to place a strong barrier between me and all ordinary marriage." Nevertheless, she felt the need to do important work, "something to prevent this sad wearing of the heart." Perhaps Mary Donaldson's idea was the answer. Yes, she thought, she would try it. "I have made up my mind to devote myself to the study of medicine," she wrote.

A medical education cost much more than the Blackwells could afford. The sisters had closed their boarding school when two of their younger brothers got jobs that paid well enough to support the family. To earn money, Elizabeth took jobs in boarding schools for girls in North and South Carolina. By day she taught music and gave piano lessons. At night she studied medicine from books in the school libraries. Meanwhile she wrote to medical schools and asked to be admitted. All of them turned her down. She applied in person to some schools in Philadelphia and New York. She was treated rudely and sometimes laughed at. Elizabeth's hopes of becoming a doctor were fading. She had applied to 29 medical colleges, and so far all the answers were "No."

Then, in October 1847, a letter arrived for her that she could hardly believe. It was from the Geneva College of Medicine. The letter was friendly and invited her to become a student there. Elizabeth was thrilled. She accepted the invitation right away. Soon she was packing her bags for the trip to upstate New York.

Why did the Geneva Medical College accept Elizabeth when every other school had rejected her? Did its professors believe in equal rights for women? Not a bit. They were also opposed to admitting a woman student. But they had a problem. Elizabeth had met a famous doctor, Joseph Warrington, in Philadelphia. She asked him to help her get into a medical school. Dr. Warrington didn't think it was a good idea and advised her to become a nurse instead. Still he admired Elizabeth for her courage. He told her that her wish might be possible. He would think about it. Finally, Dr. Warrington wrote a letter to the officials of the Geneva Medical College. He urged them to admit Elizabeth as a student.

What could they do? Could they refuse a famous Philadelphia doctor? Of course not. But maybe there was a way out. They told Dr. Warrington that they would accept Elizabeth with only one condition. Every one of the 129 male students in the class must also accept her. The officials were sure that some students would vote against her. That would solve their problem.

They were in for a big surprise. The students understood that this was just a trick. The idea was to get rid of Elizabeth and blame them. So when the time came to

The Geneva College of Medicine in the mid-nineteenth century.

vote, there was a wild scene. The students shouted, whistled, and threw things in the air. Only one student dared to say "Nay" when he voted. But when other students surrounded him, he quickly changed his vote. And that was how Elizabeth became the first woman to attend a medical college.

Her fellow students treated Elizabeth with great respect. Years later one of them, Stephen Smith, wrote about the effect she had on them. "It is quite impossible to magnify the power of Miss Blackwell over the lawless elements of that class. The moment that she entered [a room], the most perfect order and quiet prevailed." The only problems arose when Elizabeth was present during lectures on human anatomy (the study of the body). Then it was hard for the male students to remain serious. Even Elizabeth had to fight against giggling. After an anatomy class on human reproductive organs, Elizabeth wrote: "That . . . was just as much as I could bear. Some of the students blushed, some were hysterical, [and] not one could keep in a smile. I had to pinch my hand till the blood nearly came and call on Christ to keep me from smiling."

After Elizabeth graduated and became a doctor, she still needed practical experience. The place to get it was in a hospital. Philadelphia hospitals now treated her politely, but no one offered her a job. She was told to go to Paris, France. There she would find plenty of opportunities. But it wasn't so. She was turned down by one hospital after another. "The physicians of Paris," she wrote, "are determined not to grant the slightest favor to a feminine M.D." A few friendly doctors told her to disguise herself as a man, but she refused.

At last she was advised to apply to La Maternité, a hospital for women. There she would be trained to help women when they gave birth. It was not what Elizabeth wanted—her ambition was to become a surgeon. But it

A modern-day view of the Paris building that once housed La Maternité, the first hospital in which Elizabeth Blackwell worked.

was all she could get. So she agreed to work and study there for three months.

La Maternité was a dark and gloomy place. The building was surrounded by high walls, and students were not allowed outside them. Elizabeth sometimes felt like a prisoner. She worked 12 hours a day, with no time to rest. Some nights she had to work extra hours and got no sleep. But Elizabeth didn't mind hard work. She was getting good training. So she signed up for three more months at La Maternité. It was a choice that would have heartbreaking results. One day she was caring for a baby with an infected eye. While cleaning the infection, she felt a splash in her own left eye. Within hours, her vision began to go dark. There were no "miracle drugs" like antibiotics in those days. Elizabeth lay in bed for three weeks with bandages over her eyes. When the bandages were taken off, her right eye was clear. But she had no sight at all in the left. A few months later the eye became so inflamed that it had to be removed. It was replaced with a glass eye.

Elizabeth's dream of becoming a surgeon was over. But that didn't mean she would give up being a doctor. In a few weeks she was eager to get back to work again. A cousin in England helped her get a position in a famous London hospital. Elizabeth would be able to work and study in any ward and with any doctor. Only one ward was closed to her. Oddly, it was the ward for

Bloodletting, which Elizabeth's doctor prescribed for her after her eye infection, was a very common medical practice in the 1800s, but often did more harm than good. Here, a doctor administers to his patient in 1860.

Little was known about the causes and treatment of disease in Elizabeth Blackwell's time. Old and new "cures" were tried all the time. But most of them were no help at all. Some were more harmful than the diseases they were supposed to cure. Elizabeth knew it. Often she said, "Prevention is better than cure." She believed in the power of sunshine, fresh air, and cleanliness.

Elizabeth saw how her father suffered when he was dying of a fever. His treatment was calomel, castor oil, and sulfuric acid. These "medicines" caused both extreme vomiting and bowel movements. Their purpose was to "purify" his insides. Instead, they made him terribly sick. He died within a few days.

The treatment Elizabeth received when her eye became infected was also useless. Blood-sucking leeches—were attached to her head. Doctors thought the more blood they removed, the better. Hot and ice-cold cloths were placed over her eyes. Her forehead was painted with the drug opium. She was wrapped in mustard plasters and given foot baths. Her only food was broth. She lay in darkness for three weeks. Nothing worked. Later Elizabeth also tried a "water cure" in Germany.

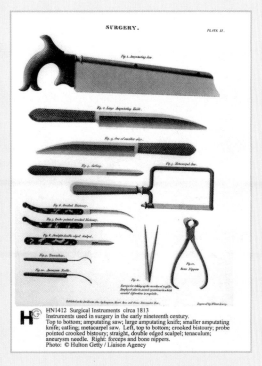

An illustration of common tools used in surgery in the early 1800s

Three times a day she was made to sweat and then take cold baths. She was wrapped in wet bandages and made to drink cold water endlessly. But the infection in her left eye only grew worse. Finally the eye had to be removed. Today, antibiotic eye drops would probably have cleared up her infection in a few days.

women who would soon give birth. The doctor in charge of this ward wrote her a note saying that "he entirely disapproved of a lady studying medicine." Elizabeth believed that he was probably afraid of losing some of his patients to a woman doctor.

While in London Elizabeth met Florence Nightingale, who later became famous as a wartime nurse. Both women believed in the importance of sanitation and modern nursing in hospitals. They became good friends for the rest of their lives.

After a year, Elizabeth returned to New York to open her own office. She was sure that she would have no problems as a woman doctor now. But she was wrong—there were plenty of problems. Landlords refused to rent office space to her. They slammed their doors in her face. People insulted her when she walked in the street. Others wrote her nasty letters. Finally a landlady did rent her office space; she charged Elizabeth much more than it was worth. Elizabeth fixed up her office, but no patients came. New Yorkers just weren't ready for a woman doctor.

What was Elizabeth to do? She began writing some lectures on health education for women. Then she rented space in a church basement and advertised in a newspaper. Today these lectures seem tame, but in Elizabeth's time people thought they were daring. She told her listeners that they must have a healthy diet and exercise.

Women were not "the weaker sex," she said. They should run, ride horses, and even wrestle. She also talked about the female body and childbirth. "I think my writing belongs to the year 1998," she joked. (It was then 1852.)

Elizabeth's lectures attracted some patients, but not enough to keep her busy. Finally she decided to open her own clinic. There, poor women would receive treatment at little or no cost. She borrowed money from friends and rented a small office in a slum area. It was soon crowded with patients. Most of them had never seen a doctor before. Elizabeth treated them in her office and in their crowded tenement apartments. She delivered their babies and cared for their sick children. She talked to them about the importance of cleanliness and fresh air.

Sometimes Elizabeth needed the advice of another doctor, but it wasn't easy to find one willing to help her. Once she asked a doctor for his opinion about an old woman who had pneumonia. The doctor became nervous. He kept saying, "I really don't know what to do!" Elizabeth couldn't understand it. He was a good doctor, and the woman was not in any immediate danger. Finally Elizabeth understood. He wasn't nervous about the old woman. He was worried about helping a woman doctor! Elizabeth kept talking to him. As soon as the doctor realized that she was a professional, he relaxed and gave Elizabeth good advice about her patient.

It was work, work, work all the time now, and Elizabeth felt lonely. She had sworn never to marry, but she did need a companion. The solution, she decided,

FLORENCE NIGHTINGALE

She was called "The Angel of Mercy." Queen Victoria of Great Britain thanked her for her heroic work. The whole nation was grateful to her. Who was this woman? Her name was Florence Nightingale, and she had a great ambition. She wanted to do something about the terrible conditions in British hospitals. They were often filthy. Bugs and mice crawled over sleeping patients. Many of the nurses were drunks. Patients died because of the bad conditions.

Florence wanted to become a nurse and improve hospitals, but her wealthy parents would not hear of it. Hospitals were not fit places for young ladies, they said. In 1850, Florence and Elizabeth Blackwell met in London. Florence admired Elizabeth for becoming a doctor. The two women talked for hours about the need to improve hospital conditions. Both agreed that cleanliness was needed to prevent the spread of diseases in hospitals. Surgeons didn't even wash their hands before operating. Their clothes were smeared with blood.

Florence got her chance in 1854 when Great Britain went to war against Russia. By now, Florence had worked in a small London hospital. With 38 other nurses, she went to the war front in Russia. She was shocked by the conditions in British army hospitals. The buildings themselves were dirty, and there

A popular view of Florence Nightingale showed her walking among her patients with a lantern. She was a beloved public figure and inspired many young women to enter the field of nursing.

were no medical supplies. Dozens of wounded men lay on the floor in rags. Florence often worked 20 hours a day to get the hospitals cleaned up. At night she would walk through the dark wards with a lantern. She did her best to make the men comfortable. Some were moved to kiss her shadow as she walked by.

After the war, she started the Nightingale School for Nurses in London. It was the first school to give professional nursing training. Florence improved the quality of nursing everywhere. Before that time, most nurses were untrained and uneducated. It was Florence Nightingale who made them skilled medical professionals.

was to adopt a child. The child she chose was a young orphaned Irish immigrant girl named Kitty Barry. "I chose her out of 400 children," Elizabeth wrote. "She wanted to come with me. . . . The poor little thing trotted after me like a dog." Elizabeth's loneliness was over. On her 35th birthday she wrote: "I feel full of hope and strength for the future. . . . Who will ever guess the restorative support which that poor, forlorn little orphan has been to me!"

It was now 1856, and a number of medical schools had opened their doors to women. One recent graduate was Emily Blackwell, Elizabeth's younger sister. Another was a Polish woman who came to Elizabeth for advice. Her name was Marie Zakrzewska (zak-shef-ska), but she was always called "Dr. Zak." It was Elizabeth's dream to open a hospital that would be run by women for women. Helped by Emily and Dr. Zak, she raised enough money to rent a house in Greenwich Village in New York City. Then she made it into a small hospital. It was called the New York Infirmary for Indigent [poor] Women and Children. It opened on May 12, 1857, in honor of Florence Nightingale's birthday. Elizabeth made a short speech on opening day. She said that women who became doctors would have to be not only as good as men but better. The idea of women in medicine was new, and its value had to be proved. Women, she said, had to prove their medical ability before expecting professional recognition.

At left: Dr. Marie Zakrzewska ("Dr. Zak") in the 1860s
At right: Dr. Emily Blackwell, sister of Elizabeth

The three women doctors—Elizabeth, Emily, and Dr. Zak—had great success. Within a few months they treated hundreds of patients. But once in a while there was trouble. One day a young woman died giving birth. Soon an angry mob formed outside the hospital. Some shouted that the doctors were killing their patients. Men armed with pickaxes and shovels tried to force their way inside. Luckily, two young policemen came upon the scene. They reminded the crowd of all the patients the women

❧ 31 ❧

WOMEN'S RIGHTS

In the mid-nineteenth century, more and more women were demanding the same rights as men. At that time, a married woman could own no property except the clothes she wore. If she inherited or earned money, it belonged to her husband. Legally he had complete control over their children. He could send them to work against her wishes. She could not sign a contract or make a will without his permission. In some ways, a single woman was better off. She could keep any money that she earned. But there were very few good jobs open to her. She might work in a factory, but the hours were long and the pay low. The best she could hope for was to become a teacher or a nanny. Most people would pity her or mock her as an "old maid."

In July 1848 a group of women met in a church in Seneca Falls, New York, to demand equal rights for all women. This convention was the beginning of an organized women's rights movement in the United States. Elizabeth Blackwell shared the goals of the women's rights movement, but she warned against going too far in its attacks on men. On her first visit to London in 1850, she said, "I cannot sympathize fully with an anti-man movement. I have had too much kindness, aid, and just recognition from men to make [this] attitude of women, [anything but] painful."

had saved. It wasn't possible for doctors to save everyone, they said. The crowd knew that the policemen were right. They calmed down and went home. The three doctors inside were able to get on with their work.

In 1861, Elizabeth moved her infirmary to a larger building. Her next goal, she said, was to start a medical college for women. But that plan had to wait. In April of that year the Civil War between the North and South broke out. Thousands of nurses would be needed to treat

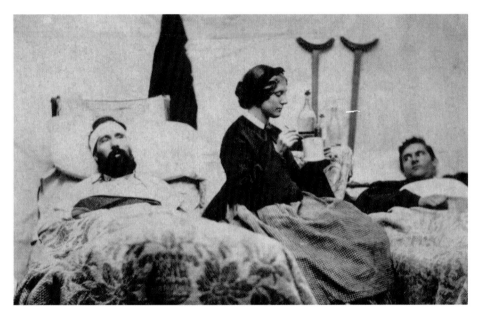

With the onset of the Civil War came the need for thousands of nurses. Following the example of Florence Nightingale, Elizabeth Blackwell, and others, women responded to the call.

wounded soldiers. In New York, Elizabeth was in charge of supplying nurses for the Union Army. So many women wanted to help! "There was a perfect mania among the women to act like Florence Nightingale," Elizabeth wrote. She sent the best ones to New York hospitals for training. Her own infirmary was one of them.

When the war ended, Elizabeth went back to her plan for a women's medical college. On November 2, 1868, her dream came true. The college, called the Women's Medical College of the New York Infirmary, opened its doors. Elizabeth could hardly believe it had happened. "It is like breathing a new and delightful atmosphere, which is nevertheless strange and dreamlike; and one almost fears to wake up with a shock."

The school began with 17 women students and 11 teachers. Elizabeth taught her favorite subject, hygiene. Emily taught about childbirth and women's diseases. There were several male teachers. One of them was Dr. Stephen Smith, who had been in Elizabeth's class at Geneva Medical College.

*M*any medical schools in the United States were now open to women. In England, however, only one woman had been able to get a diploma. "Come to England," one of Elizabeth's English friends wrote to her. "Come and help us do for women here what you have done for the women of America."

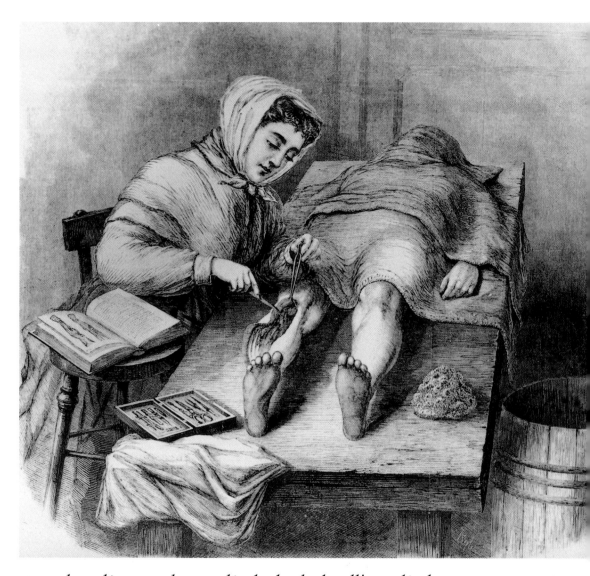

A student dissects a leg at Elizabeth Blackwell's Medical College for Women in New York City in 1870.

Elizabeth liked a challenge. She was only 48, and there was still much to do. In July 1869 she sailed for England with her adopted daughter, Kitty. Now 23, Kitty had become a valuable helper. In London, Elizabeth rented a house and opened an office. She gave many lectures on her favorite subjects. At the top of her list was the need for women doctors. The English medical profession finally gave in. In 1874, Elizabeth and two female friends started the London School of Medicine for Women.

When she was 58, Elizabeth moved with Kitty into a country cottage. It would be their home for the next 30 years. She wrote many books and articles that were published in England and the United States. The importance of cleanliness for good health was a favorite topic. She also wrote against the use of live animals in medical experiments. Laws to protect laboratory animals were not enacted until many years after her death, but she helped make them possible.

In the winter of 1876, Elizabeth wrote a book that created a sensation. It was a guide to sex education for young people, called *Counsel to Parents on the Moral Education of Their Children.* Today this book would shock hardly anyone. But in England at this time, it offended many people. A friend told Elizabeth that if her book was published, her name would be a forbidden word in England. Elizabeth wasn't afraid. She sent her book to

Kitty (right) stayed with her adopted mother for the rest of Elizabeth's life. Here they are pictured with their dogs in 1900.

twelve London publishers. Each of them said it was unprintable and turned it down. But one editor, who believed in the book, found a way to publish it. He said that it should be sent to a group of clergymen for their opinion. They agreed that the book should be published, but as a medical work. The public loved the book. It became a great success both in England and the United States.

*E*lizabeth stopped treating patients when she was 73. She was becoming weak and felt she did not have enough energy. Still, she was able at 85 to visit her family in the United States. It was a happy time for all of them. One of her nieces said, "I stood in awe of her. One felt she had conquered so much."

The next summer Elizabeth and Kitty went for a vacation to Kilmun, Scotland. They stayed at a favorite country inn. While there, Elizabeth fell down a staircase. For the next three years she seemed to be sleeping. She died peacefully on May 31, 1910, with Kitty at her side.

Elizabeth was buried at Kilmun under a white stone cross. On it was written: "The first woman of modern times to graduate in medicine (1849) and the first to be placed on the British Medical Register (1859)." British and American newspapers praised her as a true pioneer. By the time of her death in 1910, she had opened the way

COUNSEL TO PARENTS

ON THE

MORAL EDUCATION

OF THEIR

CHILDREN.

BY

DR. ELIZABETH BLACKWELL.

FOURTH EDITION.

BRENTANO BROTHERS,
5 UNION SQUARE, NEW YORK.
A. BRENTANO & CO.,
PENNSYLVANIA AVE. AND 11th ST., WASHINGTON, D.C.
LEE & SHEPARD,
41–45 FRANKLIN STREET, BOSTON.
1883.

The title page to the fourth edition of Elizabeth's sensational book, originally published in 1876. Her writing and thinking were so far ahead of their time that in 1852 she had joked, "I think my writing belongs to the year 1998."

for 7,399 women doctors in the United States alone. By 1996, the American Medical Association listed 157,387 women doctors. One out of every five doctors in the United States today is a woman.

Elizabeth Blackwell made it possible.

Important Dates

1821   February 3. Elizabeth Blackwell is born in Bristol, England.

1832   Emigrates with her family to America. They settle in New York City.

1838   Family moves to Cincinnati, Ohio. Elizabeth's father, Samuel Blackwell, dies. Elizabeth and two sisters open a boarding school.

1845   Decides to become a doctor. Teaches school and studies medicine in North and South Carolina.

1847   Moves to Philadelphia and applies to medical schools for admission. After 28 rejections, is finally accepted by the Geneva Medical College in New York State.

1849	Graduates from Geneva at the head of her class. Unable to find work in local hospitals, goes to Paris and becomes an intern at La Maternité. Becomes infected with an eye disease and loses all vision in left eye.
1850	Becomes an intern at St. Bartholomew's Hospital in London. Meets Florence Nightingale, and they become friends.
1851	Elizabeth returns to New York to begin private medical practice. Finds New Yorkers hostile to the idea of a woman doctor.
1852	Gives a series of lectures on health education for women.
1853	Elizabeth opens a clinic in Manhattan for poor women and children.
1854	Adopts Kitty Barry, a seven-year-old orphan from Ireland.
1861	When Civil War between the North and the South begins, Elizabeth recruits and trains nurses for the Union Army.
1868	Opens Women's Medical College in New York City. It is the first of its kind.
1869	Returns to England to help open the field of medicine to women there.
1874	With two other women, starts the London School of Medicine for Women.

1876   Publishes *Counsel to Parents on the Moral Education of Their Children* in England.

1894   Retires from medical practice. Continues to lecture and write on social and medical problems.

1906   At age of 85, makes her last trip to the United States to visit relatives.

1910   May 31. Elizabeth Blackwell dies.

Further Reading

Baker, Rachel. *The First Woman Doctor.* New York: Scholastic, Inc., 1944.

Blackwell, Elizabeth, Dr. *Pioneer Work in Opening the Medical Profession to Women.* New York: Source Book Press, 1970.

Brown, Jordan. *Elizabeth Blackwell.* New York: Chelsea House Publishers, 1989.

Kline, Nancy. *Elizabeth Blackwell: A Doctor's Triumph.* Berkeley, CA: Conari Press, 1997.

Wilson, Dorothy Clarke. *Lone Woman: The Story of Elizabeth Blackwell, the First Woman Doctor.* Boston: Little, Brown and Company, 1970.

Index

About the Author

Ira Peck is a retired staff writer and editor for Scholastic, where he authored many books on historical, biographical, and cultural topics. For Twenty-First Century Books, he edited *Nellie Bly's Book*, the famous woman journalist's account of her record-breaking trip around the world, which was originally published in 1890. Ira Peck lives in Mount Vernon, New York.